FOURTEEN OBSERVATIONS
OF GOOD SCRUM PRACTICE

by Carlton E. Nettleton

"I offer you Scrum, a most perplexing and paradoxical process for managing complex projects. On one hand, Scrum is disarmingly simple. The process, its practices, its artifacts, and its rules are few, straightforward, and easy to learn. On the other hand, Scrum's simplicity can be deceptive. Scrum is not a prescriptive process; it doesn't describe what to do in every circumstance. Scrum is used for complex work in which it is impossible to predict everything that will occur. Accordingly, Scrum simply offers a framework and a set of practices that keep everything visible. This allows Scrum's practitioners to know exactly what's going on and to make on-the-spot adjustments to keep the project moving toward desired goals."[1]

Ken Schwaber

TABLE OF CONTENTS

LIST OF FIGURES

Forward

Scrum is a light-weight framework for delivering valuable product to customers by empowering cross-functional, self-organizing Teams. It is uniquely balanced to enable the business to make periodic adjustments rooted in observation, feedback and empirical data. Scrum provides a framework for organizations to transform their work environments, restore a focus on the customer and reenergize their employees. The wide variation of skills, roles and experience needed for a cross-functional team to be effective gives rise to the opportunity for everyone in the organization to contribute.

The observations described in this document are practical reflections of common patterns of behavior associated with Teams and businesses using Scrum to advance their business objectives and improve employee engagement. These observations are by no means complete, or should be seen as a checklist of activities to follow, but are simply my personal guidelines to good practice.

THE SPIRIT OF SCRUM

Object

The object of Scrum is for cross-functional Team(s) of four to ten participants to regularly deliver valuable increments of working product to the business through the application of Scrum and adhering to the spirit of the framework.

Values & Principles

Success with the Scrum framework emerges from the interactions of thoughtful, dedicated individuals when their actions and words are congruent with the values and principles of Scrum. The combination of these values and principles uniquely identify Scrum and make it distinct from other frameworks.

The values which Scrum is based upon are:

- **Respect** - all participants are treated as valued, unique individuals with an important contribution to make. Each member is expected to extend this courtesy to all other individuals they encounter.
- **Commitment** - participants are expected to fully dedicate themselves to the Team, choosing to put the objectives of the Team before their own. At times, Team members may choose to make reasonable sacrifices for the greater good of the Team.
- **Trust** - participants can rely on their co-workers to perform their duties to the highest professional standards. Participants will act with positive intent and assume others are acting with positive intent as well.
- **Visibility** - nothing in Scrum is ever hidden from view. Every action, decision, artifact, outcome and conversation is freely made available to others for consideration and discussion.
- **Courage** - individuals and Teams will display strength in the face of adversity. Team members will fearlessly address issues as they arise, confident a solution can be found within their skills and abilities.

From these values, Scrum relies on these essential principles:

- **Prioritization** - periodic ordering of conflicting desires and needs is vital for success. Conversations about ranking will involve those who are affected by these decisions and take in consideration their desires and needs.
- **Accountability** - all are answerable for their decisions, words, actions and non-actions. Each person is empowered to hold one another responsible for meeting their commitments, producing quality work, following the Scrum framework and observing the Spirit of Scrum.
- **Inspect-and-adapt** - at regular intervals, the Team will check their progress and make adjustments. Scrum Teams use empirical data to drive their decisions.
- **Rhythm** - Teams will strive to develop a regular cadence to their actions. Rhythm reduces variability and increases the predictability of the Team.
- **Feedback** - participants accept and receive new information about their circumstances and environment. Feedback cycles are compressed as short as possible to amplify the effect of new knowledge and make corrections for the advantage of the business and the participants.
- **Collaboration** - beyond mere cooperation, we strive to build on top of the talents and ideas of others. Collaboration signals the shift from simply better, to astonishing business results and outcomes.
- **Self-organization** - Team members are the ones best suited to mobilize their efforts around their goals and to remain on target. Clear goals, boundaries and autonomy are necessary for this to occur.
- **Focus** - individuals will be given time and space to concentrate. Scrum strives to eliminate unnecessary interruptions so people can get things done.

Origins

The seeds of Scrum originate from a paper called "New New Product Development Game" written by two Japanese researchers, Hirotaka Takeuchi and Ikujiro Nonaka. In this paper, Takeuchi and Nonaka described a "holistic or rugby approach" to development where an entire team works on a product from beginning to end to provide greater speed and flexibility to the business. Framework co-creators, Jeff Sutherland and Ken Schwaber, borrowed the term "scrum" from Rugby Union to describe their experimental framework, born out of the process of trial-and-error, as they worked to deliver complex software products during the late 1980's to early 1990's. The first papers about Scrum were published by Ken Schwaber at the 1995 Object-Oriented Programming, Systems, Languages & Applications (OOPSLA) conference in Austin, Texas.

Theory

Scrum does not provide a complete checklist of activities, artifacts and roles to deliver a finished product. Instead, it relies on the minimum framework necessary to surface the effectiveness of your organization to iteratively deliver a product while you make improvements to your company's product development approach. Scrum is firmly grounded in three elements from empirical process control theory: transparency, inspection and adaptation. When using Scrum, thoughtful and careful individuals are allowed to guide the product step-by-step, taking regular opportunities to pause and reflect on progress-to-date. Removing, or diminishing, any one of these three elements from empirical process control - transparency, inspection and adaptation - weakens the effectiveness of Scrum.

The Scrum framework presents the maximum amount of flexibility with the minimum amount of control to help reduce and manage the complexity of modern product development by treating the "development processes as a controlled black box". When there is both a great deal of agreement between various parties on what actions to take and certainty on the cause-and-effect of our decisions, product development is not very complex and projects are thought to be "simple" (see Figure 1). In these circumstances, traditional project management techniques and tools can be applied successfully. As both uncertainty and the disagreement among the parties increases, traditional project management tools falter. In these environments, an empirical approach, like Scrum, provides a great deal of value because of the frequent realignment among the affected parties based on empirical data and feedback.

Moreover, the short time horizons employed by Scrum better link the cause-effect of decisions and increase the participants' certainty.

Application

Scrum owes much of its appeal and success when it is executed according to the principles and values of the framework, otherwise the framework is hollow and meaningless. The responsibility for ensuring this happens lies not with any one individual - it involves each person who participates and they are obligated to observe the rituals, artifacts and roles of the framework and respect the principle and values of Scrum.

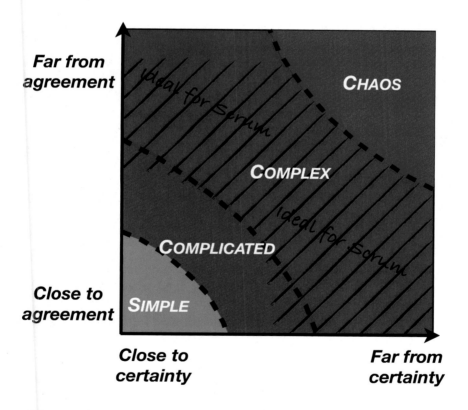

Figure 1 – Modified Stacey diagram proposing the ideal conditions for Scrum

OBSERVATION 1   THE SPRINT

1.1 Definition

The Sprint is a timeboxed iteration from one week to no more than 30 days.

1.2 Scope

(a) All activities in Scrum happen within the confines of a Sprint.
(b) Incomplete Product Backlog, or Sprint Backlog, item(s) are not allowed to cross the Sprint boundary.
(c) Sprints occur one after another, with no pauses or breaks between Sprints.

1.3 Free of distractions

(a) Once underway, the Team is given freedom and autonomy to self-manage their efforts as they work to complete their Sprint Goal.
(b) Teams may choose to pull help, advice, information and support from the surrounding organization. During a Sprint, advice, instructions, commentary and direction may not be pushed upon the Team by individuals, or groups, outside the Team.

1.4 Fixed

(a) A timebox may not be extended or contracted after a Sprint has begun.
(b) The Sprint Goal may not be altered by the Product Owner, or the stakeholders, after the Team has made their commitment to complete the Sprint Goal.

1.5 Adding & removing work items

(a) At any time, the Team has complete authority to add, remove and\or update items in the Sprint Backlog when they recognize it is out of sync with reality.

(b) If during the course of the Sprint the Team recognizes they cannot meet their commitment, together with the Product Owner they can select Product Backlog item(s) to remove from the Sprint in order to maintain the integrity of the Sprint Goal.

1.6 Finishing Early

From time-to-time, the Team may complete the Sprint Goal early. To account for these situations, the Product Owner should hold one or two small Product Backlog items in reserve. Team members may sign-up to work on these new items as long as they may be finished **completely** before the Sprint Review, i.e. they are potentially shippable and meet the Definition of Done.

If there are no items ready, or none can be completed before the timebox ends, the Team is allowed to work on tasks which interest them and provides value to the business.

1.7 Termination

(a) When the Sprint Goal no longer makes any sense given the current business conditions or after the Team provides an improved understanding of the technical constraints, the Product Owner may choose to cancel the Sprint.

(b) Any Product Backlog items that have not been started, or are incomplete, are returned to the Product Backlog.

(c) All Sprint Backlog item(s) that are Not Started or In Progress on the Task Board are wiped out.

OBSERVATION 2   DEFINITION OF DONE

2.1 Definition

A checklist of activities, standards, guidelines or conventions that each Product Backlog item must complete, in addition to the acceptance criteria, so it may be considered potentially shippable for a new, or existing, customer.

2.2 Scope

(a) The Definition of Done applies to all Product Backlog items.
(b) No Product Backlog item may be considered complete until it satisfies all the criteria outlined in the Definition of Done.
- (i) A completely done Product Backlog item includes all the necessary analysis, design, programming, refactoring, testing, reviews, documentation and approvals required for a feature, or deliverable, to be considered complete in your organization.
- (ii) Testing includes unit, system, user, regression, acceptance, performance, security, stability, integration and stability. Definition of Done also includes any internationalization, as required by the product.
(c) Product Backlog items which do not meet the Definition of Done may not be demonstrated at the Sprint Review.

2.3 Creation

(a) The Definition of Done is the result of a negotiation between the Team, the Product Owner and the various stakeholders representing the business. The ScrumMaster facilitates this conversation.
(b) Regardless of the wishes, desires and hopes of the Product Owner, ScrumMaster and the stakeholders, the Team has the final word on what is included in their Definition of Done.

2.4 Maintenance

(a) No one may change the Definition of Done once the Team has begun a Sprint.
(b) The ScrumMaster, Product Owner, any Team member or any stakeholder may suggest additions or deletions to the Definition of Done.
(c) The Team has the final authority to accept or reject any changes to the Definition of Done. Changes take effect in the following Sprint.

2.5 Enforcement

(a) Responsibility to enforce the Definition of Done lies with the Team alone.
(b) If the ScrumMaster feels a Product Backlog item does not meet the Definition of Done, they are obligated to inform both the Team and the Product Owner.

OBSERVATION 3   THE PRODUCT BACKLOG

3.1 Definition

A prioritized list of the functional and non-functional requirements necessary to develop and launch a successful product. It is a living document that reflects an evolving understanding of the product, the customers and the market.

3.2 Ownership

The Product Backlog is owned and prioritized by the Product Owner alone.

3.3 Product Backlog Item

Describes a single feature, function, technology, enhancement, bug fix or deliverable expected for the product. It describes what the Team must build and why it is valuable to the business.

Every Product Backlog item should have a clear acceptance criteria and is estimated by the Team.

3.4 Creation & Maintenance

(a) Any individual and\or member of the Team may suggest features to add to the Product Backlog, but the Product Owner has the final say if the item will be included in the Product Backlog.
(b) The Product Owner and the Team are expected to reserve time each Sprint to prepare, analyze and review upcoming Product Backlog items before the next Sprint Planning meeting.

3.5 Prioritization

(a) Product Backlog items are ordered by business value, from highest value at the top to lowest at the bottom.

(i) Every Product Backlog item must be ranked.

(ii) No item may have the same ranking as another.

(b) Any individual and\or member of the Team may offer advice on how to prioritize a Product Backlog, but the Product Owner has the final say how the item will be prioritized relative to existing Product Backlog item(s).

3.6 Size

Product Backlogs that are comprehensible and manageable normally contain from sixty to one hundred items.

(a) When there are many small Product Backlog items, the Product Owner may bundle them into larger Product Backlog item(s).

(b) If Product Backlog grows beyond one hundred items, the Product Owner is allowed delete the lowest priority item(s) from the list.

(c) If no one can remember why an item is valuable, the Product Owner is allowed to delete it from the Product Backlog.

3.7 Tending the Product Backlog

Product Backlog items are progressively refined and decomposed just-in-time to minimize rework and eliminate waste. An item is sufficiently decomposed when the acceptance criteria is clear and the Team can provide an estimate.

(a) As an item increases in priority, the Product Owner and the Team analyze the item and decompose the item into chunks of work that can be completed within a Sprint. This process may create new Product Backlog items.

(b) As Product Backlog items which have dependencies with other Teams, or have business and\or technical risk, rise to the top of the Product Backlog, the Team and Product Owner may choose to analyze and decompose these items in more detail.

3.8 Release

A collection of Product Backlog items that will be delivered by a specified date or with a defined scope.

(a) A release is divided into a series of three to ten Sprints which allow the business the maximum number of opportunities for feedback, adjustment and learning before the product is delivered to the customer.
(b) Product Backlog items for a release are sequenced according to business value.
  (a) Items with the highest business value are scheduled earlier than items with lower business value.
  (b) Items with the highest business value are guaranteed to be delivered, while items with lower business value have the potential to be dropped from the release.

3.9 Release Burndown Chart

(a) The Product Owner will create and maintain a graph showing the remaining amount of estimated work versus the number of Sprints in the release (see Figure 2).
(b) The Release Burndown chart is updated when Product Backlog items are added, removed and\or an estimate is updated. At a minimum, the Release Burndown chart must be updated twice during a Sprint.

READING A RELEASE BURNDOWN CHART

Figure 2 shows a sample Release Burndown chart for a Team with eight Sprints in their release. At the start of the release, the Team estimated 130 units of work would be delivered in eight Sprints. At the end of Sprint #1, they delivered twelve units of work (the green bar) and 118 units remained (the red bar). As the release progressed, a little more of the Product Backlog was delivered by the Team in the next two Sprints.

In Sprint #4, the scope of the release increased by thirteen units (the yellow bar) and the Team only completed three units of added functionality. In the figure, one can see the velocity of the Team increased during Sprints #5 and #6, completing twenty and twenty-one units of work, respectively.

At the end of Sprint #6, it was clear the scope of the release was too large for the Team to complete before the deadline. The Team's velocity of twenty-one units per Sprint and the concept of Yesterday's Weather, indicated the Team would not burndown all the remaining work before the end of Sprint #8.

As a result of this data, twenty-five units of low business value Product Backlog items were dropped, or descoped, from the release by the Product Owner. When Sprint #8 was completed, nine units of work remained, but it had marginal business value. Since the remaining work provided little benefit to the business, they chose to ship the product on time and within budget. The remaining work was returned to the Product Backlog for prioritization in the next release.

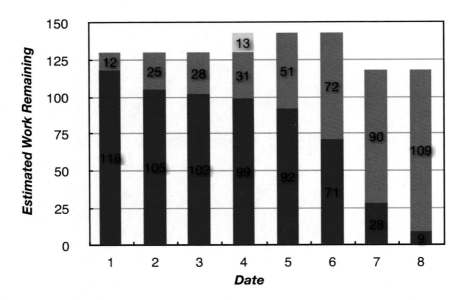

Figure 2 - Sample Release Burndown chart for an eight Sprint release

OBSERVATION 4   THE TEAM

4.1 Definition

Dedicated collection of self-organizing, interdependent, co-located individuals representing different functional roles with all the necessary skills to turn Product Backlog items into a potentially shippable increment within the Sprint.

4.2 Authority

- (a) Members of the Team are self-managing with respect to their day-to-day activities.
  - (i) Team members are entitled to select the work which matches their abilities and interests.
  - (ii) Any member of the Team can refuse a work assignment.
- (b) Team members are empowered to modify their work environment in order to improve their communication, collaboration and happiness.
- (c) If a skill, or a useful tool, is absent from the Team and this absence hinders the Team from achieving their Sprint Goal, or delivering the product, Team members are authorized to take steps to fill the gap.

4.3 Responsibilities

- (a) Commit to and self-organize around the Sprint Goal within the context of the organization while observing both the Scrum framework and the Spirit of Scrum.
- (b) Collaborate and share their knowledge, experience and perspective with other members of the Team, the Product Owner, ScrumMaster and the business.
- (c) Help other members of the Team when asked and ask for help when they are stuck.
- (d) Look for ways to improve themselves and the performance of the Team.
- (e) Help create and maintain the Sprint Backlog, Sprint Burndown chart and Task Board.
- (f) Assist the Product Owner with analyzing and decomposing

Product Backlog items.

(g) Regularly demonstrate working product at the Sprint Review.
(h) Implement action item(s) identified during the Retrospective.
(i) Facilitate Sprint Planning, Daily Scrum and Retrospective meetings when the ScrumMaster is unavailable, or when requested by the ScrumMaster.
(j) Attend all Scrum meetings on time and prepared.

4.4 Commitments

Each member of the Team is responsible for their own commitments and should only make commitments they truly feel they are going to fulfill.

(a) No person in Scrum may make a commitment on the behalf of another.
(b) No member of the Team should feel pressured to make a commitment based on the over commitment of another.

4.5 Size

Scrum Teams range from six to eight individuals plus or minus two.

4.6 Membership

(a) Any person who is responsible for delivering a work product in service of the Sprint Goal is considered a Team member. If they have hands on a keyboard, they are part of the Team. If they merely have advice to give, they are considered stakeholders.
(b) Scrum Teams are persistent and long-lasting. Team composition remains stable during a Sprint. Apart from true emergencies, members are normally added or removed at Sprint boundaries only.
  (i) Any Team member may choose to leave the Team for a different Team better suited to their needs.
  (ii) The Team can choose to expel a Team member who is unproductive or violating either the Spirit of Scrum

or the framework.

4.7 Titles

There are no titles on a Team other than Team member.

4.8 Multiple Teams

A Team member is assigned to only one Team at a time.

4.9 Rights

Every Team member has the following rights:

(a) To produce quality work at all times.
(b) To know what is needed from the business with clear declarations of priority.
(c) To ask for, and receive, help from peers, management, and customers.
(d) To experiment with new ideas, technologies and roles to grow both as a professional and an individual.

OBSERVATION 5   THE PRODUCT OWNER

5.1 Definition

An empowered individual applying their personal and professional judgment to make decisions in the best interest of different, often times competing, business stakeholders to maximize the business value the Team produces each Sprint.

5.2 Authority

Only the Product Owner can set the priorities for the Team.

5.3 Responsibilities

(a) Maximize the business value delivered by the Team through any means necessary.
(b) Maintain and prioritize the Product Backlog by tending the Product Backlog regularly.
(c) Support the ScrumMaster in helping the Team become self-organizing.
(d) Regularly provide reports to the stakeholders about the progress of the product.
(e) Clearly communicate and impart the business case for the product to the Team and stakeholders.
(f) Learn about the business's needs and understand how the product improves the business.
(g) Identify and build relationships with the different product stakeholders.
(h) Be a good steward of corporate resources and support the Team members by obtaining any resource(s) they might need.
(i) Create and maintain the Release Burndown chart.
(j) Guide and steer the product using the tools available to Scrum.
(k) Help the ScrumMaster with organizing the Sprint Review meeting.
(l) Attend all Scrum meetings on time and prepared.

5.4 Delegation

While the Product Owner may choose to delegate activities, i.e. analysis, interface design, end user interviews, testing, etc., they can never delegate their responsibility to maximize business value.

5.5 Business Value

Describes all forms of worth which determine the health and well-being of the company in the long-run.

This includes, but is not limited to, profit, market share, knowledge gained, waste reduction, time to market, productivity, social impact, risk, growth, customer satisfaction, employee satisfaction, quality, market differentiators and other factors relevant to the organization.

5.6 Maximizing Business Value

The Product Owner is responsible for both the long-term and short-term decisions which affect increasing the business value of the product. He\she must always be asking *"What will provide the highest impact to the business now?"*

This requires a certain degree of flexibility, adaptation and risk taking. A Product Owner will regularly reorder the Product Backlog to opportunistically respond to the emerging needs of the product, stakeholders, business and\or market.

5.7 Multiple Teams

(a) A novice Product Owner should only be responsible for a single Team.
(b) A skilled Product Owner should have no more than two Teams.

5.8 Rights

Every Product Owner has the following rights:

(a) To receive the greatest possible value out of every week.
(b) To know what can be accomplished by the Team, when and at what cost.
(c) To see incremental progress in a viable product proven to work by passing acceptance criteria they specify.
(d) To be informed of schedule changes promptly in order to take effective countermeasures and reset expectations with the stakeholders.
(e) To collaborate with the business on setting the future direction of the product.

OBSERVATION 6   THE SCRUMMASTER

6.1 Definition

A dedicated individual responsible for improving the performance of the Team and the business by any means necessary.

6.2 Authority

The ScrumMaster is a recognized expert on the Scrum framework and its application. Yet, the ScrumMaster has no authority over the day-to-day activities of the Team, the Product Owner, the stakeholders or the business.

6.3 Responsibilities

(a) Teach the Team, the Product Owner, the stakeholders and the organization how to use Scrum to maximize business value.
(b) Preserve the integrity of the Scrum framework and maintain the Spirit of Scrum.
(c) Ensure the Team remains focused on the work before them.
(d) Make impediments visible and work with others to remove them.
(e) Look for ways to improve themselves, the performance of the Team and the flow of value through the business.
(f) Collaborate and share their knowledge, experience and perspective with other members of the Team, the Product Owner and the business.
(g) Communicate the value of Scrum with other stakeholders in the business.
(h) Help other members of the Team when asked and ask for help when they are stuck.
(i) Facilitate Sprint Planning, Daily Scrum, Sprint Review and Retrospective meetings.
(j) Create the Task Board and Sprint Burndown chart at the start of every Sprint.
(k) Attend all Scrum meetings on time and prepared.

6.4 Balance

A ScrumMaster must always be looking to strike the right balance between enhancing the Team and the helping improve the flow of value through the organization. A ScrumMaster who spends too much time and effort looking to the Team, will cultivate a business environment that does not appreciate the value of Scrum. If too much time is spent looking out at the business, the performance of the Team will suffer as they revert to familiar patterns of behavior.

The precise ratio a ScrumMaster spends working with the Team and spends improving the larger organization depends on the skills of the ScrumMaster, the maturity of the Team, the complexity of the product and the nature of the business environment. As a Team matures in it's self-organization, the ScrumMaster will spend more of their time working with the business to reduce waste and improve flow. Even as the Team matures in it's ability to self-organize, a ScrumMaster should remain attached to a Team to preserve their focus and accountability to deliver results.

6.5 Accountability

The ScrumMaster is empowered to hold the Team, the Product Owner and the stakeholders accountable for their commitments. It is their obligation to respectfully reflect when a person's actions and\or words are inconsistent with their commitments, Scrum and the Spirit of Scrum.

The same standards and level of accountability which the ScrumMaster applies to the participants of Scrum, also apply to the ScrumMaster.

6.6 Respect

While the ScrumMaster is never satisfied with the status quo and continually working with the Team and the business to find and implement improvements, they must do so with the utmost respect and care for the people they work with. A ScrumMaster should remember their efforts are dedicated to helping others grow and realize their fullest potential.

6.7 Multiple Teams

(a) A novice ScrumMaster should only be responsible for a single Team.
(b) A skilled ScrumMaster should have no more than two Teams.

6.8 Rights

Every ScrumMaster has the following rights:

(a) To try out different ideas, approaches and techniques to remove impediments which impede the flow of value.
(b) To be given time for initiatives to take hold and produce change.
(c) To take measured risks and learn from setbacks.
(d) To be supported by senior leaders in the organization.
(e) To be provided access to different parts of the business while identifying and removing impediments.

SCRUM ROLES ARE BALANCED

It is important that each role in Figure 3 is filled. The Product Owner is concentrated on the providing valuable business outcomes to the business, while ScrumMaster is aiming their efforts at the execution of good Scrum and improving the flow of value to the customer. Meanwhile, the Team remains centered on learning how to self-organize and deliver potentially shippable increments regularly. Stakeholders provide feedback on the value of everyone's efforts.

When Scrum falters, it is often because people are not committing to their roles. Other times, organizations chose to overload one, or more, roles in a single person, disrupting the balance of the roles. Recall, the Scrum framework was designed to provide the maximum amount of flexibility with the minimum amount of control. If these roles cannot be filled with individuals who will fully inhabit them, or they are overload, the control mechanisms of Scrum become unhinged, visibility is diminished, accountability is lost and the framework loses its meaning.

When Scrum is done well, there exists a natural tension between each role. This tension exerts a force that tends to prevent the other roles from meddling in responsibilities that are not their own. Since there are considerable gray areas on the role boundaries in Scrum, each role will eventually bump into one another as they discover what are the boundaries of their responsibilities. This friction is an essential part of learning how to do Scrum and making it meaningful to your business. Through the of process of inspect-and-adapt, the precise definition of each role - Team member, Product Owner, ScrumMaster and stakeholder - emerges as your organization gains experience using Scrum.

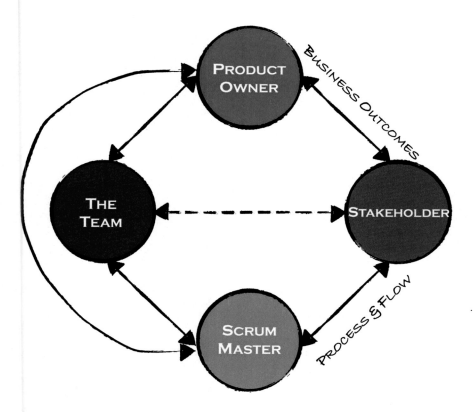

Figure 3 – Relationships between the various roles in Scrum

OBSERVATION 7   SPRINT PLANNING

7.1 Definition

A timeboxed meeting at the beginning of each Sprint for the Team and the Product Owner to negotiate on what the Team will deliver and demonstrate at the Sprint Review.

7.2 Format

(a) The Sprint Planning meeting shall not exceed eight hours.
  (i) During the first half of Sprint Planning, the focus of the conversations between the Product Owner and the Team discuss **WHAT** Product Backlog items the Team will build.
  (ii) In the second half of Sprint Planning, the conversation shifts to the Team as they talk through **HOW** they are going to build the product by decomposing the Product Backlog items into Sprint Backlog items.
(b) Sprint Planning is facilitated by the ScrumMaster.

7.3 Attendees

(a) The Team members, Product Owner and ScrumMaster are required to attend Sprint Planning.
(b) Subject matter experts, stakeholders, end users and other knowledgable parties may be asked to attend all, or part, of Sprint Planning when their expertise is needed by the Team.
(c) Stakeholders and other interested parties are welcome to attend from time-to-time.

7.4 Sprint Goal

(a) The Product Owner is expected to provide a unifying theme which summarizes the business value the Team is expected to provide at the end of the Sprint.
(b) The Sprint Goal should connect all the selected Product Backlog items and be comprehensible to a knowledgeable stakeholder or business leader.

(c) The Sprint Goal is the standard on which the Team and Product Owner are evaluated by the stakeholders and the business.
    (i) The Team is evaluated on their ability to deliver the Sprint Goal within the timebox of the Sprint while maintaining quality and flexibility to the business.
    (ii) The Product Owner is evaluated on the business value the Sprint Goal provides the organization and accurately translating the business needs into a working product.

7.5 Scope

The Team should plan to complete three to eight Product Backlog items each Sprint.

7.6 Work Assignments

(a) Each Team member selects the Sprint Backlog item(s) that interests them and writes their initials on the item to indicate they are responsible for completing the work.
    (i) Team members can select all the items they are going to work on during the Sprint at Sprint Planning or they may choose them one at a time from the remaining unfinished items on the Task Board.
    (ii) Team members may trade Sprint Backlog items between one another during a Sprint.
(b) It is the responsibility of the Team to ensure the work is fairly and evenly distributed across the Team.

7.7 Commitment

The purpose of Sprint Planning is to help the Team understand if they can commit to delivering the Sprint Goal by the close of the timebox. Once the Team commits to the Sprint Goal, they are held accountable for delivering a potentially shippable increment that fully conforms to the Definition of Done.

(a) The only commitment the Team makes is to the Sprint Goal.
    (i) The Team makes no commitments to complete

specific Product Backlog item(s) nor specific Sprint Backlog item(s).

    (ii) The Team shall not under commit nor overcommit, but strive to improve their ability to estimate their capacity accurately.

(b) If the Team feels they cannot commit to the Sprint Goal, the Product Owner shall remove Product Backlog item(s) until the Team can commit fully to the Sprint Goal.

(c) The ScrumMaster is empowered to hold the Team and the Product Owner accountable for any commitment(s) they make during Sprint Planning.

OBSERVATION 8   THE SPRINT BACKLOG

8.1 Definition

A list of all the tasks identified by the Team representing their current understanding of how they plan to achieve the Sprint Goal.

8.2 Ownership

The Sprint Backlog is owned and maintained by the Team alone.

8.3 Sprint Backlog Item

A single task, activity, or deliverable, defined and estimated by a Team member.

8.4 Creation & Maintenance

(a) All Team members are expected to contribute and estimate the tasks that make up the Sprint Backlog.
    (i) Team members may work as individuals, subgroups or as one large group to identify and estimate the tasks.
    (ii) Tasks should range from four to sixteen hours to provide visibility and focus.
(b) Any Team member may add or remove items to the Sprint Backlog.
(c) Any Team member may update an estimate for a task in the Sprint Backlog.

8.5 Sprint Burndown Chart

(a) The Team will create and maintain a graph showing the amount of estimated work remaining versus the number of days in the Sprint (see Figure 4).
(b) The Sprint Goal is the title of the Sprint Burndown chart.
(c) The Sprint Burndown chart must be updated at least once a

day prior to the Daily Scrum.   Preferably, the Sprint Burndown chart is updated when Sprint Backlog items are added, removed and\or an estimate is updated.

8.6 Role of the Sprint Backlog

Since the Team makes a commitment to the Sprint Goal, all the Sprint Backlog items and estimates are irrelevant.

However, the Sprint Backlog performs a crucial service for the Team.   It is the artifact that assists the Team with self-organizing around work, to take responsibility for delivering the product and offers visibility.   Without the Sprint Backlog, the Team could not inspect-and-adapt since this artifact provides the raw materials for the Sprint Burndown chart and the Task Board.

8.7 Reporting

The Sprint Backlog is an artifact for the Team to inspect-and-adapt their work.   It is offered in the spirit of openness, not as in invitation for micromanagement.

USING A SPRINT BURNDOWN CHART

A Sprint Burndown chart is a simple tool used by the Team to provide a measurement on how close they are to meeting the Sprint Goal by the end of the Sprint. When a Sprint Backlog item moves from In Progress to Done on the Task Board, it's estimate is removed from the total estimated work remaining in the Sprint. When new Sprint Backlog items are discovered during the course of a Sprint, their estimates are added to the total estimated work remaining on the day the new item was identified by the Team.

There are four common patterns in most Sprint Burndown charts. The sample chart in Figure 4, based on real Sprint data from a 2010 Scrum Team, displays all of these patterns.

1. The Sprint Burndown goes flat, as seen on Days #4 and #5.
2. The projected trend (or slope) has the Team completing the Sprint after the timebox expires, as shown between Days #6 and #7.
3. New work is added late in the Sprint, as indicated on Day #6.
4. A large delta between the actual progress of the Team and the predicted progress of the Team (as if they had burned down an equal amount of work each day), as seen between Days #5 to #9.

In all these cases, these patterns provide an opportunity for the Team to discuss what is really going on and provide an explanation. If the Team is confident they can still fulfill the Sprint Goal regardless of how the data is displayed in the Sprint Burndown chart, the Product Owner and the ScrumMaster should always respect the judgment of the Team. Recall, the Team commits to delivering the Sprint Goal at the Sprint Review, not to deliver the Sprint Backlog items.

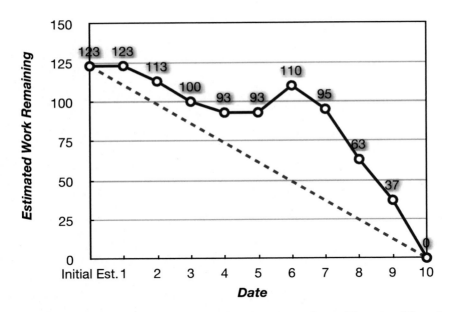

Figure 4 - Sample Sprint Burndown chart for a Team with a ten day Sprint

OBSERVATION 9   DAILY SCRUM

9.1 Definition

A daily, timeboxed gathering for the Team members to reconnect with one another, reaffirm their commitments to one other and make adjustments to meet the Sprint Goal. The Daily Scrum is not a problem solving meeting or a status report.

9.2 Format

(a) The Daily Scrum is a timeboxed meeting not to exceed 15 minutes.
    (i) Once the timebox has expired, the meeting is over, even if all the Team members have not spoken.
    (ii) The timebox may be extended for a specific allotment of time, i.e. five more minutes, only by the unanimous consent of the Team.
(b) Daily Scrum meetings are held at the same time, space place each day.
(c) The Daily Scrum is facilitated by the ScrumMaster, or a member of the Team.

9.3 Attendees

(a) The Team members and ScrumMaster are required to attend each day.
    (i) If a Team member cannot attend, they are responsible to make arrangements for their personal account to be communicated to the rest of the Team.
    (ii) If the ScrumMaster cannot attend, a Team member will facilitate the Daily Scrum.
(b) While not required to attend, the Product Owner should be available to attend the Daily Scrum on most days.
(c) Stakeholders and other interested parties are welcome to attend from time-to-time. The Team has the authority to exclude any non-Team member from the Daily Scrum if their comments are disruptive, dilatory or not adding value to the Team.

9.4 Three Questions

Every person who attends the Daily Scrum, including any visitor, is expected to provide answers to the following questions:

1. What did you do yesterday?
2. What will you do today?
3. What is blocking your progress?

9.5 Meeting for Meetings

During the Daily Scrum, Team members, Product Owner, ScrumMaster or stakeholders may raise topics, concerns or issues, that are of interest to all, or part, of the Team. The Daily Scrum is the opportunity for those people who are interested in the topic to connect and make arrangements for a second conversation some time after the Daily Scrum concludes. It is the responsibility of the parties interested in the topic to make that meeting happen, not the ScrumMaster.

OBSERVATION 10   SPRINT REVIEW

10.1 Definition

A timeboxed meeting at the end of each Sprint for the stakeholders and other members   of the business to provide the Product Owner and the Team feedback on the product and their progress to date.

10.2 Format

(a) The Sprint Review is a hands-on demonstration of the working product by the Product Owner and the Team.
   (i)   The Sprint Review begins with a brief overview of the Sprint Goal and the selected Product Backlog items.
   (ii) The Product Owner and the Team demonstrate the completed functionality, note any deviations from the Sprint Goal and Product Backlog items and receive feedback from the stakeholders and the business.
   (iii) Stakeholders and other parties are encouraged to explore the product and be active participants in the demonstration.
(b) The Sprint Review is facilitated by the ScrumMaster.

10.3 Attendees

(a) The Team, Product Owner and ScrumMaster are required to attend.
(b) The Product Owner is responsible to ensure the stakeholders impacted by the functionality delivered attend.
(c) All other interested parties are welcome to attend.

10.4 Deliverables

(a) Only working product may be demonstrated at a Sprint Review.
   (i)   Documents and other intermediate artifacts, such as architectural diagrams, use cases, workflows, user interface design documents, specifications, test

cases, coding standards, requirements documents, user manuals, etc., may be used as supporting elements to a demonstration of working product. They are **NEVER** the central focus of the Sprint Review.

    (ii) The working product must be demonstrated in an environment which mirrors the customer's environment.

(b) Only Product Backlog items that meet the acceptance criteria and the Definition of Done may be demonstrated.

10.5 Unfinished Work

Unfinished work is any Product Backlog item(s) that does not meet the acceptance criteria and\or fails to fully conform to the Definition of Done. Incomplete work is not demonstrated at the Sprint Review since it gives the stakeholders the illusion of progress and diminishes their ability to inspect-and-adapt.

(a) The Team receives no "partial credit" for unfinished Product Backlog item(s).

(b) It is at the discretion of the Product Owner if an unfinished Product Backlog item is prioritized for the next Sprint.

(c) No unfinished Sprint Backlog item(s) may rollover into the next Sprint.

10.6 Outcomes

Any number of outcomes are possible after a Sprint Review:

(a) Continue to the next Sprint with no changes.

(b) Reprioritize the Product Backlog based on feedback from the stakeholders, the business, customers and\or end users.

(c) Release the demonstrated functionality to customers.

(d) Delete Product Backlog item(s) based on changing business conditions.

(e) Add new Product Backlog item(s) based on feedback from the stakeholders, the business, customers and\or end users.

(f) Reformulate the Team by adding or removing members, including the Product Owner and\or the ScrumMaster.

(g) Add more Team members (or Teams) to increase the pace.

(h) Stop further investment in the product by disbanding the Team.

OBSERVATION 11   RETROSPECTIVE

11.1 Definition

A timeboxed meeting at the end of each Sprint for the Team to reflect on their progress, provide feedback to one other and inspect-and-adapt.

11.2 Format

(a) This meeting is a conversation between the Team members.
(b) The ScrumMaster will facilitate the Retrospective.

11.3 Attendees

(a) The Team, Product Owner and ScrumMaster are required to attend.
(b) Attendance by any visitor is by invitation only.

11.4 Topics

The Team can use the time allocated for the Retrospective to discuss any topic that will help them improve the product, the organization, the Team, their skills, interpersonal dynamics, or even the Scrum framework. They may reflect on the past, the present or discuss the future.

(a) Topics are selected by the ScrumMaster based on their observations of the Team, Product Owner, stakeholders and the business environment.
(b) The Team may override any topic selected by the ScrumMaster.

11.5 Action Items

(a) The Team is responsible for capturing and implementing any action item(s) which may arise.
(b) The ScrumMaster is empowered to hold the Team, and individuals, accountable for any commitment(s) they make

during a Retrospective.

11.6 Reporting

The Team owns the information generated at the Retrospective. Only the Team has the authority to share this information with others.

11.7 Role of the ScrumMaster

The Retrospective is for the Team.

The ScrumMaster is present to establish a sense of safety, ensure a balance of viewpoints is provided and that each member of the Team is allowed to contribute. While the ScrumMaster may have opinions and ideas on how the Team should improve, he\she should not substitute their judgment for the Team's.

THE FOCUS OF SCRUM

The complete workflow of the Scrum framework is illustrated in Figure 5. There are two key concepts vital to understanding how Scrum works.

1. Feedback is the engine that drives Scrum and occurs at multiple levels on multiple time horizons.
2. Scrum produces two deliverables of equal importance to the business: improved product and improved business capability.

Nearly every piece in the framework is designed to provide the participants feedback. In the Daily Scrum, the Team is given feedback on their progress-to-date. The Sprint Review provides the Team, Product Owner and stakeholders feedback on the value of product and changing business conditions. During the Retrospective, the Team gives themselves feedback on how well they are working together and what needs to improve in the organization. Each Sprint gives feedback on the viability and relevance of the Vision. Every piece of feedback is used to inspect-and-adapt. As a result, adjustments can be made so the organization can respond to change.

When the time between cause-and-effect is delayed, no learning will occur because the accountability for a decision taken in the distant past is weak. On the other hand, if feedback is too rapid, the organization is overwhelmed with the noise of change and cannot make sense of the learnings the Team is providing. Therefore, it is essential to select Sprint lengths, which provide maximum opportunities for feedback. Every business and industry has different forces acting on how rapidly feedback can be accepted, but because Scrum is action-oriented there is a preference for shorter timeframes. Keep in mind that dampening, or removing, feedback loops in Scrum hobbles the framework and puts your business at risk.

In every Sprint the participants of Scrum produce two deliverables for the business: the product and improved ability by the Team to deliver high-quality work to the customers faster. Both deliverables are key to supplying value fast to the customers. Removing one, or focusing on one at the expense of the other, unbalances the Scrum framework and reduces it's effectiveness by producing local optimizations. These local optimizations are toxic to Scrum.

In many cases, Scrum Teams quickly get started and make rapid improvements. Work that floundered for weeks, gets delivered in a Sprint or two. Teams that were once disengaged and lethargic, display a great deal focus and renewed purpose. These rapid improvements stem from the inspect-and-adapt cycle brought on by the Retrospectives and rekindled feelings of ownership and accomplishment. However, in the course of improving their capability, many Teams run afoul with organizational standards, procedures and policies, which inhibit them from reaching greater levels of productivity, improved delivery of business value and increased personal satisfaction. When these larger organizational impediments are repeatedly identified, escalated to management and not acted upon, many Team members become disinterested in making additional sacrifices for change. Many Team members come to recognize the only people being asked to change are themselves and that change stops at management's door. Avoid this pattern or Scrum will be just another meaningless management fad in your organization.

Scrum is an extremely pragmatic tool for thoughtful and caring participants to adjust their product development process via short cycles of experimentation using their powers of observation and empirical data. The balanced deliverables of Scrum furnish the business with plenty of feedback, rich opportunities for learning and a framework to amplify learning across the organization. All of these combine together to improve the workplace and achieve competitive advantage in the market.

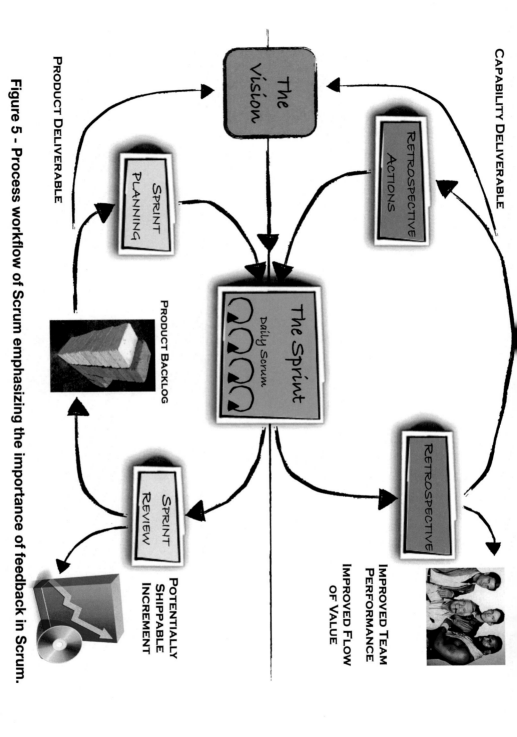

Figure 5 - Process workflow of Scrum emphasizing the importance of feedback in Scrum.

Observation 12   Stakeholders

12.1 Definition

Any person who has a direct, or indirect, interest in the work of the Team.

12.2 Authority

A stakeholder has no direct authority on the Team.

However, due to their role in the organization, a stakeholder may wield a great deal of influence over the Team's environment, norms, standards and Definition of Done.

12.3 Responsibilities

(a) Provide candid feedback directly to the Team at Sprint Reviews.
(b) Attend Sprint Planning meetings when their expertise is requested by the Team.
(c) Regularly work with the Product Owner to define and fine-tune the Product Backlog.
(d) Remove impediments identified by the Team, Product Owner or ScrumMaster.
(e) Avoid distracting the Team after the Team has committed to the Sprint Goal.
(f) Support the Scrum framework.

12.4 Rights

Every Stakeholder has the following rights:

(a) To receive regular status updates through interacting with a working product.
(b) To change their mind, substitute functionality, and adjust priorities without paying exorbitant costs.
(c) To cancel the product at any time and be left with a working product providing real business value reflecting the investment to date.

OBSERVATION 13   SPRINT TERMINATION MEETING

13.1 Definition

A timeboxed meeting to understand why a Sprint was canceled and prevent a cancelation from occurring again.

13.2 Format

(a) This meeting is a dialogue to identify the root cause(s) of why a Sprint was canceled.
(b) The ScrumMaster will facilitate a Sprint Termination meeting.

13.3 Attendees

The Team, Product Owner, ScrumMaster and affected stakeholders are required to attend.

13.4 Action Items

(a) The participants have a responsibility to communicate the key learnings discovered during the Sprint Termination meeting to the rest of the business and implement any recommended countermeasure(s).
(b) The ScrumMaster is empowered to hold the participants accountable for any commitment(s) they make during a Sprint Termination meeting.

13.5 Timing

The Sprint Termination meeting should occur soon after a Sprint is terminated.

OBSERVATION 14   TASK BOARD

14.1 Definition

A visual control used by the Team to inspect-and-adapt, foster teamwork and help them complete the Sprint Goal.

14.2 Format

(a) A Task Board is a physical artifact in the workplace.
(b) It is composed of the selected Product Backlog items, the Sprint Backlog items and the Sprint Burndown chart.
(c) There are only four states for an item on the task board: Not Started, In Process, Done and Blocked.

14.3 Creation & Maintenance

(a) After Sprint Planning, the ScrumMaster will set-up the Task Board for the Team.
(b) The Team is permitted to modify the layout of the Task Board provided by the ScrumMaster and to add, or remove, states to suit their needs for self-organization, communication and visibility.
(c) Team members are responsible for updating the Task Board each day.
(d) Only the Product Owner can move a Product Backlog item to the Done column.

14.4 Blocked Items

Items which are Blocked are re-assigned to the Team member best able to resolve the blockage now.

14.5 Limiting Work-in-Progress

To eliminate queues, reduce waste and increase the flow of value, the Team should be mindful to watch how many work items are being executed simultaneously.

(a) To increase the likelihood of meeting their commitment, The Team should strive to have no more than two Product Backlog items In Process at one time.

(b) To limit context switching, each Team member should strive to have no more than three Sprint Backlog items In Process at one time.

(c) To minimize delays and encourage flow, the Team should strive to have no more than one item Blocked at a time.

PURPOSE OF THE TASK BOARD

A Task Board, as shown in Figure 6, is an information radiator used by the Team to stimulate collaboration, cross-functional behavior and true ownership of the work. It is extremely powerful in helping the Team with self-organization and their ability to inspect-and-adapt because it puts intangible product development work in plain sight and makes the flow of work between Team members visible. The real-time data provided by the Task Board challenges Team members to become empowered actors in the development process. It's presence prompts them to resolve issues as they occur, rather than act as detached participants waiting for someone to fix issues or resolve dependencies for them. The Task Board is a passive mechanism to remind the Team they own the work and hold each other accountable.

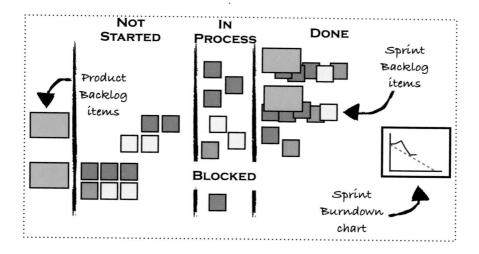

Figure 6 – Sample layout for a simple Task Board.

DEFINITIONS

Blocked: status of a work item on the Task Board that has encountered an impediment and is waiting in a queue for resolution.

Burndown Chart: the trend of work remaining across time in a Sprint, a release, or a product. The source of raw data for this graph is the Sprint Backlog and\or the Product Backlog, with work remaining tracked on the vertical axis and the time period (days of a Sprint or Sprints) tracked on the horizontal axis.

Business Value: all forms of worth which determine the health and well-being of the company in the long-run.

Customer: the originator of value; the entity which will purchase and\or use the product.

Definition of Done: a checklist of activities, standards, guidelines or conventions that each Product Backlog item must complete, in addition to the acceptance criteria, so it may be considered potentially shippable for a new, or existing, customer.

Done: status of a work item on the Task Board that is complete.

Emergent: arising and existing only as a phenomenon of independent parts working together, and not predictable on the basis of their properties.

End User: any person who operates the product.

Flow: the movement of value toward the customer.

Functional (requirement): description of a specific behavior the product should do when completed; explains what the product should do.

Greater Good: the benefit of more people than oneself.

Impediment: any obstacle that inhibits the flow of value to the customer.

Increment: product functionality that is developed by the Team during a Sprint.

Information Radiator: a physical display in the workplace showing people information they care about without having to ask anyone a question.

Iteration: one cycle within a project. In Scrum, this cycle is called a Sprint.

In Progress: status of a work item on the Task Board that is actively being worked on by the Team.

Non-functional (requirement): criteria used to judge the operation of the product; explains how the product should be.

Not Started: status of a work item on the Task Board that is waiting to be developed.

Positive Intent: belief that individuals want to make things better and they care to do the right thing.

Potentially Shippable: a completed increment that has the possibility to be delivered to a customer should the business choose to exercise this option.

Product Backlog: a prioritized list of the functional and non-functional requirements and features for the product.

Product Backlog Item: a single feature or user need for the product.

Product Owner: individual responsible for understanding the business needs, ordering the Product Backlog to deliver maximum business value and communicating status to the stakeholders regularly.

Queue: sequence of work items held in temporary storage awaiting completion.

Scrum: a mechanism in Rugby Union to restart a dead ball. Scrum is not an acronym.

ScrumMaster: responsible for unlocking the potential of the Team, removing any roadblocks which inhibit the Team from routinely delivering business value and guardian of the Scrum framework.

Sprint: a timeboxed iteration not to exceed 30 days.

Sprint Backlog: a collection of tasks which represent the Team's current understanding of how they plan to achieve the Sprint Goal.

Sprint Backlog Item: a single task, activity, or deliverable defined and estimated by a Team member.

Sprint Goal: a short summary describing the Product Backlog items the Team commits to complete during the course of a Sprint.

Stakeholder: any individual who is interested in the output of the Team, but does not have responsibility to complete any tasks.

Task: a single work item needed to complete the Sprint Goal.

Task Board: a visual control used by the Team to inspect-and-adapt, foster teamwork and help them complete the Sprint Goal.

Team: a group of people who commit to delivering the Sprint Goal and responsible for completing the Sprint Goal by the close of the Sprint. While the ScrumMaster and the Product Owner are distinct roles in Scrum, they are considered part of the Team.

Tending: the process of reviewing and progressively refining upcoming Product Backlog items before the next Sprint begins.

Timebox: a fixed length of time that neither expands nor contracts from Sprint-to-Sprint.

Unit: dimensionless quantity of work.

Value: anything of worth that the customer will pay for.

Velocity: the pace at which the Team converts estimated Product Backlog items into a potentially shippable increment.

Vision: description of why the project is being undertaken and what the desired end state is.

Visual Control: are means, devices, or mechanisms that are designed to manage processes by making the problems, abnormalities, or deviation from standards visible to everyone, providing immediate feedback to people and conveying timely and useful information.

Waste: anything the Team, or the business, does or

produces that the customer will not pay for.

Yesterday's Weather: empirical observation that a team with a fixed membership and fixed iteration length will deliver about the same output at the end of the current iteration as they delivered in the previous iteration.

CITATIONS

1 Schwaber, K., 2003, Agile Project Management with Scrum: Microsoft Press.

2 Takeuchi, H. and Nonaka, I., 1986, New New Product Development Game: Harvard Business Review, **64**, 137-146.

3 Schwaber, K., 1995, Scrum Development Process *in* J. Sutherland, D. Patel, C. Casanave, J. Miller, and G. Hollowell, eds. Business Object Design and Implementation, OOPSLA 1995 Workshop Proceedings: Springer.

4 Adkins, L., 2010, Coaching Agile Teams: Addison-Wesley.

REFERENCES

Adkins, L., 2010, Coaching Agile Teams: Addison-Wesley.

Beck, K. and M. Fowler, 2001, Planning Extreme Programming: Addison-Wesley.

Cohn, M., 2010, Succeeding With Agile - Software Development Using Scrum: Addison-Wesley.

Jeffries, R., A. Anderson and C. Hendrickson, Extreme Programming Installed: Addison-Wesley.

Larman, C. and B. Vodde, 2008, Scaling Lean & Agile Development: Thinking and Organizational Tools for Large-Scale Scrum: Addison-Wesley.

Poppendieck, M. and T. Poppendieck, 2003, Lean Software Development, An Agile Toolkit: Addison-Wesley.

Schwaber, K., 1995, Scrum Development Process in J. Sutherland, D. Patel, C. Casanave, J. Miller, and G. Hollowell, eds. Business Object Design and Implementation, OOPSLA 1995 Workshop Proceedings: Springer.

Schwaber, K., 2003, Agile Project Management with Scrum: Microsoft Press.

Stacey, R.D., 1996, Strategic Management and Organizational Dynamics: The Challenge of Complexity: Prentice Hall

Takeuchi, H. and I. Nonaka, 1986, New New Product Development Game: Harvard Business Review, **64**, 137-146.

Rugby is a good occasion for keeping thirsty bullies far from the center of the city. .

~ Oscar Wilde ~

Made in the USA
San Bernardino, CA
19 October 2016